HUMAN EXTINCTION

THE IGNORED THREAT

A brief common-sense look at what overpopulation is,

where it is taking us, and how we can correct it.

MICHAL H. HALL

This book is dedicated to my wife Linda,

without whose encouragement, input and assistance

none of my books would ever have been

written or published.

Contents

INTRODUCTION

Let me begin by telling you how I evolved to write this book. I was brought up by caring, intelligent parents who encouraged me to grow in my understanding of everything. My parents endured criticism for seeking justice and equality in everything. Early on they supported the civil rights movement, and I always admired them for that, My father was a professor of philosophy and religion, so I was attuned to deep discussions of ethical concerns. I began my own education with a college, masters, and doctors degree, and I chose to make my contribution as a Presbyterian minister. I served numerous churches for over forty years. This allowed me to begin eight large organizations to meet human need. I then stepped back to launch myself into a period of powerful learning and evolution. I spent the first four years researching and studying everything I could find on world religions and the new scientific discoveries. I became especially attracted to the knowledge coming from recently translated scriptures of the world's religions and the amazing explosion of knowledge in cosmology. I soon found that I had to turn loose of a multitude of previously held assumptions in order to be true to my ever evolving search for truth.

I started writing mainly to help me understand the things I had found, and make them a part of who I am. I then wrote several books which I used in teaching, and I've recently published three books called <u>The Absurdity of Pride and the Peace of Humility,</u> <u>The Cosmic Way,</u> and a story called <u>Rediscovering the Earth</u>. They all reflect my cosmic, interconnected, world wide perspective, and my ever evolving search for truth. This book came out of my shock at seeing that there are two glaring truths right in front of us that are totally being ignored. Nobody ever talks, or seems to care, about our stored and ready to explode hydrogen bombs, or our shocking overpopulation of the Earth to bring about our quick extinction. As we wallow in our shallow escapes to ignore them, nothing is being done about them...and nothing will be done.

In writing this, I am continuing my search for truth. For instance, I have come to see us as a deviant, lost species that will quickly go extinct. I believe that is because we have chosen the divisive arrogance of pride over uniting humility and love.

This has led us to discard our mother planet Earth as we selfishly pollute its air, water and land, kill off its animals and plants, and destroy its ecosystems in which all living beings exist. This pride and arrogance has also led us away from patiently understanding each other to become murders on the streets of our cities and in our insane wars. We see ourselves as especially chosen, privileged life forms that were put here by a human-like, mythological figure in the sky. This has led us to believe that we are over, and in conrol, of everything, and this leaves us pridefully evolving into chaos. We pridefully think that our mythical gods will do whatever we want, and that they will even even prevent us from dying. Pride has also trashed all of our individual, group, and species relationships. This leaves us divided and alone as we compete in the divisive misery of violence and war. It also leaves us covering-up the shocking truth that our species is quickly going extinct!

I have recently observed that a huge player in our drift into extinction is the *growing population of our species on the Earth.* If you are not aware of this, it›s not surprising. Most people are so lost in their own need, greed, money and massive escapes that they shrug off everything but themselves. They certainly ignore this very real problem by saying it's just not true. Other people say that the divine myth, in which they were raised, has created us and will deal with it all. Regardless of what you think, I would urge you to read this. I believe we should all learn more about overpopulation before we come to our final conclusion. You will see that our overpopulation of the Earth (which has happened in just over one hundred years) is crazy! It is multiplying our abuse of the Earth and its ecosystems to dramatically speed up our species fall into extinction. That is what this book is about.

I.

OTHER WAYS THAT WE COULD GO EXTINCT

It is appalling to me that so few people know that there are things going on that could make us extinct. Many times when I am talking about overpopulation, I make this statement, and almost every time that I do, someone stops me and says they didn't know that we might go extinct.. Then they ask if I can tell them what these things are that might lead us to it. Therefore I would like to take a few minutes to list the ones that I'm aware of. I'm doing this in case when you start to read this, you ask the same question. Some of these things are more familiar than other and ;also more accepted than others. However all of them could destroy us. Some of them we know a lot about, but others like overpopulation, we know almost nothing about.

1.

We know for instance that **asteroids** have plummeted the Earth leaving huge craters since the Earth's beginning. We also know that a major asteroid strike can wipe out most of the life-forms on the Earth, because that has happened several times before. We've seen this recently in the strike that came at the time of the dinosaurs to wipe them, and most of life on the Earth, away. Thus it is true that at any time an asteroid could hit the Earth. However now we are able to track them. Also following many studies and meetings that discussed what we could do to avoid a strike, we now have strategies to divert a large, problematic asteroid. They found that to blow them up would just send out shot-gun pieces of rock that could destroy things even more, so they have now developed plans to divert and move them away with atomic blasts. Rockets to carry the bombs into space have successfully been tested and are ready to go when a threat is found and affirmed. This means that this threat of extinction for us is now very minimal.

2.

The invention of bombs came from the invention of cannons and planes. They became the most effective way to kill. However they inspired something much bigger. Most of us are aware that an **atomic bomb** was dropped in World War II. After hearing that a laboratory in Berlin had discovered nuclear fission, on December 28,1942, President Franklin D. Roosevelt authorized the Manhattan Project that brought scientists together to do nuclear research. Thus in Los Alamos, New Mexico, the development of an atomic bomb began under the direction of J. Robert Oppenheimer. Then on July 16, 1945, under the name of the Trinity Test, the first atomic bomb was successfully detonated. It created a mushroom cloud over 400.000 feet high. In July 1945, Harry Truman called for Japan to surrender promising 'prompt and utter destruction" if this did not happen. On August 6, 1945, the United States dropped the first atomic bomb from a B-29 on the Japanese city of Hiroshima. It leveled five square miles of the city and killed over 80,000 people. Later tens of thousands died from radiation exposer. Then on august 9, a second bomb was dropped on Hiroshima killing around the same number of people. Atomic bombs come from fission reactions. However now we have developed an immensely more powerful thermonuclear bomb that comes from the rapid release of energy during the nuclear fusion of an isotope of hydrogen. A **hydrogen bomb** uses an atomic bomb as its trigger. Fortunately this bomb (sometimes called a suicide bomb) has never been dropped on a city. Nine countries claim to have conducted hydrogen bomb tests. They are United States, Russia, United Kingdom, China, France, India, Israel and Pakistan. Recently North Korea has claimed to have done so. There have been many attempts to make sure that this monstrous weapon is never used. However as more nations are able to make these bombs, the risk of human stupidity and error rises...and the risk of our extinction from them grows.

3.

Although it is obvious, and has been accepted by most scientist, far fewer people are aware of another threat to our extinction. It could just be called **pollution,** and we will address it in more detail later. However I will discuss it now because it is only when we break it down into its many parts that we be able to understand it:

    A. Air pollution, which exploded into view when industrialization started using unsustainable, fossil fuel. Also coal, together with car, truck and airplane emissions, have filled our atmosphere with so many toxic elements that our lungs are now struggling to serve us. Lung diseases and respiratory problems like asthma and chronic obstructive pulmonary disease, acute lower respiratory infections, lung diseases and lung cancer constantly haunt us. Air pollution also causes many of our strokes and cardiovascular problems, and it is also a threat to pregnant women and newborns. I will discuss later the subject of global warming from the H2O from coal and oil, but I must say that I am always shocked by those who are still denying it. The green-house effect from these things has been proven over and over. It is accepted by essentially all scientists. It is a threat to the coasts and islands of this planet as it melts the arctic regions. It is dramatically affecting the ecosystems to wipe away many plants and animals. It is causing devastating changes in our weather to elevate fires, storms, hurricanes, and other things with its warming.

B. Fresh water pollution is destroying drinking water all over the world. Although laws have been passed to stop individuals and companies from dumping waste into rivers and streams, there is still far too much of it around.

C. The pollution of the *oceans* is not talked about because it's so horrible! Things like the oil from ships and pleasure boats, the dumping of garbage, nuclear waste, sewerage and plastic are never discussed. Many say marine life will be gone in 50 years.

D. Land pollution is also ignored, and I believe it's the worst of all. Sure there are garbage and garbage dumps on the land, but that's the least of it. For instance land pollution clearly has to do with our greed and selfishness in paving over more and more of the land, clearing off vast areas of shrubs and trees to try to feed the growing billions of people, building more and more structures to make more towns, cities, and megalopolises. We also spray the land with poisons, increasingly burn it up with global warming, and wipe-out the necessary rain forests without ever thinking about or appreciating what they are doing for us. I call all of this "murdering the land" because we are destroying it without mercy.

E. Plastic is taking over the world. Why...because it is not biodegradable. This type of pollution never breaks up to enter the Earth the way most other things do. When it's made, it stays. Recently I saw a published report from "Seas at Risk" that talked about the disposable plastic use across Europe. They reported 46 billion plastic drink bottles, 16 billion coffee cups with plastic lining and 36.4 billion plastic drink straws. We've started using plastic for almost everything. We use it on our houses, our boats, our furniture, our cars, our utensils, and on and on. Smaller things like plastic bags, cups, bottles, holders and other junk are thrown out to go into landfills, but they can never become a part of the land. They are also throw onto the side of roads and into ditches to be washed into lakes and rivers and finally the oceans. Marine life is threatened by plastic as they try to eat it or get tangled in it. The great streams of the oceans are producing gigantic, swirling plastic junk piles all over the world.

4.

All of this pollution is also impacting something that most people know very little about. It is something we call the Earth's **ecosystems**. They are the way that all animals and plants have evolved, and now should be evolving, to survive. It is the biological outer layer of the Earth's surface. Nature (or natural) evolution has evolved to provide a balanced food chain and proper environment for the survival of all life-forms. For instance, this involves the availability of plant and animals for food, but it also requires the existence of a nurturing surrounding. This includes things like temperature, water, the height, the depth, and many other things, They all allow various life-forms to exist. Even though humans are different in that they can quickly adjust to different ecosystems, other animals and plants cannot. If they are to survive, they must live in the same environment of their birth. They must eat the same food in the same temperature and surroundings. In other words, they must live only in one ecosystem. However Humans are presently destroying more and more of the Earth's ecosystems as they destroy the water, and land, as well as the animals, plants and marine life. Of course since these are all things that we desperately need to survive, we are destroying ourselves as well. Our destruction of the ecosystems is also assuring our extinction.

Though all of this is right in front of us, we refuse to look at it. We're too busy burying ourselves in silly escapes. However I do think that the things I've mentioned above are at least sometimes acknowledged. I've found that most people know that these things exist. However, what if there is something just as bad, or perhaps even worse, that none of us have ever contemplated or even heard, that is equally devastating for our future? Suppose it is something that right now is totally ignored? That is what this book is about. That is why you need to read it!

II.

WHAT IS OVERPOPULATION?

Overpopulation simply means there are way too many Homo sapiens on the Earth. Of course we have to ask how could that happened? Well the population rose very slowly at first, but then, all of a sudden, it took off like a rocket! I'll begin by giving you some expert estimates on the world's population up to 1750, and then I'll give you reports after that from the UN data sheets:

In 70,000 BC there were 1 thousand, 500 people on the Earth.

In 10,000 BC there were 4 million.

In 8,000 BC there were 5 million.

In 5,000 BC there were also 5 million.

In 4,000 BC there were 7 million,

In 3,000 BC there were 14 million.

In 2,000 BC there were 27 million.

In 1,000 BC there were 50 million.

In 500 BC there were 100 million.

In 1 AD there were 200 million.

In 1,000 AD there were 400 million.

In 1500 AD there were 458 million.

In 1600 AD there were 580 million,

In 1700 there were 682 million,

In 1750 AD there were 791 million,

In 1800 AD there were 1 billion,

In 1850 AD there were 1 billion 262 million.

In 1900 there were 1 billion 262 million.

In 1950 there were 2 billion 525 million.

In 1975 there were 4 billion 61 million.

In 2000 there were 6 billion 127 million.

In 2010 there were 6 billion 930 million.

In 2015 there were 7 billion 349 million people on he Earth!

Now remember, our species is 200 thousand years old. Thus **it took us 130** *thousand* **years to reach 1. 500 people. It then took us 26** *thousand* **years to reach I billion. However t***he* *shocker is that it took us just <u>1 hundred</u> years to reach a popu-lation of over <u>6 billion people</u> existing on the delicate ecosys-tems that sustain life on the Earth!* *Think about this, because that last statistic **is totally insane!*** You can see how our population has very quickly grown out of control. It has been estimated that **The Earth can only sustain 750 million** of a single species. What are we doing? *How could this be happening? How could we allow this to happen?* Hear are some answers that I have found that might help to explain this madness:

A. The Vicious Cirle of More Children Having More Children

Our population is out of control for many reasons. The first is totally obvious. Part of the problem is that in the past, humans needed many children to help the parents survive, and this was exacerbated by the fact that most of these children died in their first two years. Also a man would have several wives because so many women died in childbirth. Thus if he needed many chil-dren he needed to marry over and over, which of course meant that it was expected that men would have several wives, and even have them at at the same time..

The problem is that now only a very few people need to have several children, but many people are continuing to do so. This means that the population keeps on growing and growing. The more people there are to have children in one generation, the more people there will be in the next generation to have children, and this makes the population explode. It's a vicious circle of growth in the human population that can never stop. It's not hard for us to see that having more and more children is the main reason that overpopulation has occured.

B. Constantly Improved Medical Care

Obviously as medical care has improved, more people have lived longer...and the population has grown. The average age in 1800 was 30, but now it is 80. New discoveries in medicines and trained medical professionals have changed our approch to illnes and disease to constantly heal millions of people. Before we had the evolution of medical education, illness was addressed by practicioners of various superstitions or religions. This is a complicated subject but I offer some of what I've found on the history of this life saving change:

1. Early medical traditions evolved in Babylon, China, Egypt and India.

2. The Greeks intoduced medical diagnosis, prognosis and medical ethics (for instance the Hippocratic Oath was written in Greece in the 5th cenetury BC).

3. In medieval times, surgical practices were improved and systematized in Rogerius <u>The Practice of Surgery</u>.

4. Universities began systemic training of physicians around 1220 in Italy.

5. During the Renaissance, understanding of anatomy improved, and the microscope was invented.

6. The germ theory of disease in the 19th century led to cures for many infectious diseases.

7. Military doctors working in wars began advancing methods for both trauma treatment and surgery.

8. Public health measures were developed in the 19th century to address the rapid growth of cities with sanitary problems.

9. The 20th century exploded with medical improvements. It saw advanced research centers opened that were often connected to new, sophisticated hospitals.

10. The mid-20th century evolved new biological treatments, such as antibiotics. This paralleled many other

      developments in chemistry, genetics, and lab technologys (such as x-rays). All of this led to what we now call "modern medicine".

11. As the rights of women grew in the 20th century, it opened up new careers for women as nurses and even physicians (1970).

I could go on with this but the point is that as more and more people are saved from diseases, they live much longer, and as infant mortality rates go down, the population grows dramatically. World-wide figures on all of this are difficult to find because records were often not kept, and also because different parts of the world have mortality rates resulting from things like differeent cultural mores, and standards of living. Still I believe it's clear that equally significant to the vicious circle of our population growth through childbirth is *the ability of medicine to save lives and allow people to live much longer*. Clearly medical advancement has dramatically contributed to our present overpopulation of the Earth.

We must remember that overpopulation comes when there are too many of any one species (in this case humans) in the ecosystems. It occurs when too many of one species upsets the delicate balance of the interconnected reality that *each being in an ecosystem depends on all the others in that system.* Any imposed imballance of this amazing work of nature, such as overpopulation, can cause death and finally the extinction of any or all of the species that live within an ecosystem.

People have often said to me that we can't be going extinct because there is still so much "space" left in this world. They say that all we need to do is spread out. I point out to them that, even though many of the areas they are talking about are uninhabit-able (like deserts, mountain tundra, the arctic, antartic, etc.), *they are totally missing the point!* The problem has nothing to do with space; it has to do with *the destruction of the ecosystems* that sustain all life on the Earth! This means that we are intimately tied to all of the other animals and plants in our ecosystems. If any one species swarms out of control in an ecosystem to over-use, eat up, pollute, or drastically alter it, then that species has to go. It's natural (nature). The guilty species will face increasing, countless problems, and it is forced out by the Earth in order to support its other, compatable species. That is what is happening now to us. We are grossly abusing the ecosystems in which we live, so the reality is...we must go!

This picture of our extinctinction is agreed upon by many environmentalists, but the timing of our departure is another thing. Some say that we will be gone as early as 100 years, but I would agree with many others that it will be within 200 to 300 years...but of course nobody knows because no one can predict the future. What we do know is that at some time far too soon, the clean air, fresh water, availabile food from plants and animals, fertile land, clean oceans, and much more, will all be erased. All of that involves our overpopulation that is now speeding-up our pollution, violence and wars, which will consistently get worse as people fight for their survival. The Earth will go on and recover from our damage, but we will appropriately be gone.

Why is Overpopulation Being Ignored?

In the light of all of this, why would a supposedly intellegnet species insist on ignoring our overpopulation? Why would we not be altering our actions to preserve the ecosystems and save ourselves, and most of the rest of life, on this Earth? Why would we rush to our own extinction?

This is an important, huge question, because I believe that what is now happening in the world literally makes no sense. It does appear that we have cracked-up. We see this blind, nervous breakdown in politics around the world, in the way we ignore global warming, in our lack of support for the United Nations to allow more and more stupid and tragic wars; we see it in overpopulation with its many problems; and we see it in our in pollution of everything, It's clear to me that the cause of our insanity has nothing to do with something simple that we are constantly talking about. No, it is something much more complicated. It has to do with something that is right now altering our natural evolution on the Earth. It has to do with some things that are basic, deep and very powerful. It must be things that are so horrible that they turn us away from a sensible, sustainable relationship with the Earth to throw away our future.

I have written several books around the fact that we are going extinct. I have recently written two books that I believe help us to answer the question of why overpopulation and our pending extiction is being ignoreed. They were entitled The *Absurdity of Pride and The Peace of Humility* and *The Cosmic Way.*

A. Our Choice of Pride Over Our Natural Humility

In my first book it had become clear to me that as a species we will soon be extinct, but I went on determined to find the cause. I discovered that it is caused by our selfishness, pride, arrogance or greed. It comes from any number of words that refer to a seperating emotion that says that we, or things associated with us, are *the best!* I found that this way of thinking has taken us over to enslave us, ruin our lives, and drive us into extinction. I also found the word that I felt most comfortable calling it...is pride.

I broke it into three obvious groupings. ***Individual pride*** destroys our personal relationships to leave us alone and angry. ***Group pride*** destroys our relationships with other nations, religions, races, sexes, or any other groups that are different from our own. This seperating emotion, power (or whatever you want to call it) tears us apart into disgusting violence and war.

The first two of these forms of pride makes us miserable, however the third one is even more serious. Clearly the worst of these is **Species pride** that alienates us from our fellow species and also alienates us from the Earth itself! It is this form of pride that is driving us into extinction as we kill off the other life forms arounds us, pollute the air, water and land, and even destroy the ecosystems that sustain all of life. Also this divisive pride (where we have evolved to worship greed, money and progress) is the major reason *why we continue to overpopulate* to speed-up our estinction. It helps us to destroy the Earth and those coming after us.

B. Deserting The Cosmic Way

The second book I've published also recognizes pride's evil presence, but it goes on to ask *how* we have allowed ourselves to evolve into this divisive state. In my studies of science, I found that evolution moves forward as things *come together* to be more complex...to be something more. A simplified example of this is when, after the Big Bang, we see that quarks, leptons, and bosons came together to form atoms; atoms came together to form molecules; molecules came together to form cells; cells came together to form organs, bodies and ultimately the most complex thing of all...brains. I also saw that this "moving together to be more complex" is not just basic to the evolution of the cosmos, but since we are a part of the cosmos, it's basic to *our evolution* too. If we want to continue evolving into the cosmos, we have to be coming together rather than constantly moving apart. When we choose something that *tears us apart*, that might be described with words like arrogance, pride, and greed we are not evolving. No, we are de-volving. When we choose this, we choose it over what I call "The Cosmic Way" that brings us together. It is described by words such as humility, love and peace. Thus since what we are choosing now is moving us apart, we will seperate and de-volve into fear, hate and violence. We are also continuing to ignore the needs of our fellow animals and plants to destroy the ecosystems as we increasingly overpopulate the Earth. All of this causes us to become more and more polorized and hostile, and soon we will leave after a disastrous struggle for survival.

One day in my studies, I found that all of the world's religons came together in Chicago to form what is now called "The Parliament of Word Religions". They gathered to searh for the things that they agreed on. They eventually found that they all agreed on the necessity of things like love, humility, kindness, justice, forgiveness, sharing, giving, peace, and other things that *unite us and bring us together*. Aspects of these uniting concepts are found in almost all religions, but they are also found in other things like our conscience, our teachings on ethics, our writings in poetry and prose, and in everyday, common-sense, life experiences, However, in our actions, we have clearly ignored these things . We may sometimes nod in their direction, but we then turn around and vigorously embrace divisive pride with its arrogance, self-centeredness and greed to totally wipe out the uniting emotions. When we do experience the uniting emotions that offer us a meaningful life now, as well as a future, it is often said that we are being naieve, weak, uninformed, a bleeding heart, radically liberal, or much worse. In my book, I call this uniting, sustaining force of the cosmos *"The Way"* because that's what some of the founders of the world religions called it. For instance, it's what Jesus, The Buddha, Lao-tzu, and many others called it. I also call it The *Cosmic* Way because of its association with the way that everything comes together in the cosmos. Thus choosing pride over The Cosmic Way is why we selfishly continue our overpopulation of the Earth. It blinds us to the fact that our overpopulation is a huge player in our pending extinction.

C. Escaping Reality

We have become an escapist species. In most of the world today, much more time is spent in trying to escape reality than in living in it. Thus the feeding of these endless escapes has become big business! For instance, we escape the results of our human divisions with things like religions and superstitions, alcohol and drugs, television and movies, sports and recreation, constant work to make more money than we need, and on and on. Our divisive, competitive, dog-eat-dog pride in our money-making cultures has left us isolated, lonely and depressed. It is natural that we respond to this by trying to get away...by tryng to escape. We try to escape most things like our failures, our losses, our miserable lives with our insane wars, persecutions, injustices, starvations, and on and on. We are even trying to escape the obvious fact of global warming, and the fact that our species is going extinct. People have lost their interest in things like truth, justice, happiness and peace to entertain themselves with stories about division, violence and war. We have no interest in pursuing what is real. We bury ourselves in television and movies of nonsense, together with sound-bites of prejudice, meanness and violence. We retreat into a past that never existed and blindly lose ourselves in things like sports, making more money, and arguing politics. Is it any wonder that faced with a society gone mad, we are also ***escaping the obvious fact of overpopulation?***

There is no question that the subject of overpopulation is not just hard for us to address, but it is also complicated and sometimes difficult to understand. Other things easily block it out. For instance we have been taught to "be fruitful and multiply"... and we have certainly done that! Also overpopulation is blocked out by things like religions, governments, laws, economics and our assumptions about sex, marriage, family. All of these things contribute to why we ignore overpopulation...which is anything but an escape. No, unfortunately overpopulation is a real irresponsible frightful fact!

Also, the fact is that overpopulation really does frighten people. Sometimes it can even make them mad or angry. When

I've talked about this, I have seen where this subject would threaten people's past assumptions so much that they would become so agitated that they stand up and leave. It has become clear to me that the reason that overpopulation is being ignored is because multiplying our species is deeply embeded in who we are. It is seen as where we have evolved to be and do. To change this will be extremely hard because it must first require us to see that we are quickly going exctinct...and that is certainly not pleasant . We must then be willing to look honestly at the dramatic mental, and even physical, changes that will be needed to stop overpopulation and save our mother Earth!

IV

What Will Happen if We Keep Ignoring Overpopulation?

If someone is able to see that overpopulation is true, and then, in their love for those coming after them, and their love for their species, join in sounding the alarm and even work for change, it will not be easy! To even talk about it is going against the grain and not making friends. Sure, the easiest thing to do is to just wrap-up in all of our massive escapes to selfishly ignore the future and go through life ignoring this powerful truth. History reveals over and over where people have ignored injustice and cruelty in things like slavery, As well as the abuse of people of color, other nationalities, other religions, the handicapped, minorities, women, gays and many more. That is bad, however if everyone ignores overpopulation and the abuse of the Earth, it will mean that there will be no meaningful evolution ahead of us in which we can move forward. Instead we'll be stuck in the mud of the often untruthful, mindless status quo. Overpopulation is different from the other problems we've faced, because it has a time-line that is running out. If we can't see the reality of overpopulation and respond to it quickly, overpopulation will so speed up our human extinction that it will soon be on top of us. Of course if that happens, our species, our future, and our place in the cosmos will vanish. Humans will disappear to be no more! Here are some *specific* things that will happen if we ignore overpopulation:

A. Over-crowding

This first one is obvious. Every time we go to a city, town, beach, or other highly populated area, we are embroiled in people, cars, trucks, and traffic-jams. If you have not experienced this, it just means you've never go anywhere.

I once talked with an elderly woman in Asheville, North Carolina who told me how much Asheville had changed since she was a little girl. She began each sentence with "When we didn't have all these people." She talked about how she could remember when everyone knew each other and were concerned about each other. She told about driving into town without ever slowing down. She said that the people waiting on her in the stores were friendly people she knew. They were either the owners of the store or someone in the owner's family, She said that she knew them, and they knew her. She told about how safe, and how much fun, it was to go downtown in those days. I remember how she shook her head and said, "There are just too many people here now...way too many people". I had found Asheville not to be as crowded as other places I had lived, so I was surprised by what she said. I think this was one of the first times my eyes were opened to overpopulation and what it is doing to us.

Even though all of us, if we think about it, experience some of overpopulation's problems, this is nothing to what will soon follow. There will be so many people that traffic will become intolerable, the downtown of cities will be impassible, and housing will be impossible. There will be so many people struglling to survive in unimaginable crowded conditions that nobody will will be able to tolerate anybody. In other words, living standards will deteriorate into distrust, disrespect chaos and misery.

This has been scientifically observed when too many mice have been put in the same cage. Shortly after, they start fighting with each other to the point of injury. Too many of any species in the same place causes chaos, and we as a species are no different. Even now we can see people getting more and more separated, angry, and violent as the population grows. What will it be like in two hundred years?

B. Horrible Relational Problems

As a highly evolved species, we need relationships. In fact our complex reflective brains leave us needing relationships much more than other specires. We have individual relationships (with each other), group relationships (with other groups of people), and we should have species relationships (with the Earth and its many other species) but we don't at all. If we ignore the reality of overpopulation, it will progressively harm all of these relation-ships even more. Our relationships will crumble under overpop-ulation's weight to leave us and the world in divided chaos. You and I both know that to some extent this is already happening. We can see it.

I recently saw a documentary on the most remote island in the world called Tristan de Cunah. It is 2,090 miles from South America and 1,500 miles from South Africa and has 262 inhabitants. It is self sufficient and only five small ships come with any provisions each year. The interesting thing to me is that this documentary found that its peope had evolved to work together with each other in things like planting potatoes, fishing and other things. They became very aware of protecting and preserving the land, the water and the fish. They were also seen sharing everything. When asked about it they said it was because they realized that it just made sense. They were also found to be a peaceful, kind, and happy population who were totally content with their surroundings. I bring this up to say that a small population of people cannot only survive on their own, but they can live peaceful and rewarding lives. On the other hand, we are constantly proving that over-crowded, competing, prideful people live violent, destructive, miserable lives.

The cosmos teaches us to come together, but we, in our prideful overpopulation that ignores the Earth and its ecosystems, are *not* coming together. No, we are gradually falling apart, and as our population continues to grow, it will get much worse. Even though we have talked about some of these things before, let me give you *some examples of what is happening* that are very hard to hear...but listen to them anyway because I believe they are true!

1. Family Disintegration

As more and more people fight for the things that are necessary (which many of us now take for granted), the pressure on families will grow. For instance problems with being able to find enough food to feed the masses will effect every family in their struggle to survive. Divorce in the world is presently going up every year partly because of the stress of making money. How much greater will that stress be when jobs have all but disappeared, competition is brutal, food is scarce or gone, land and housing are beyond reach, vacations are nonexistant, toxic air, rivers and oceans are the rule, and angry people fighting with each other are everywhere? Will this help to stabalize marriages, or help in the raising of children? The family unit, that is usually the most lovng, caring, secure, stable and safe place to be, will be threaened and eventually may dissolve. I know that all of this is hard to take in because we now take so much for granted, however a planet over-run by a viral, mean, overpopulated species can alter and eventually destroy their quality of life...even within the family unit as we know it.

I also believe that overpopulation, together with computers, I-pads and I-phones are limiting our children's relationships with each other and the Earth (which speeds-up our pending extinction). This is happening because before overpopulation exploded in upon us around one hunded years ago, children were allowed to move freely through their neighborhoods and beyond to play with friends. Now all of that is changing. It's happening because more and more people hear reports about crime, so more people get tense and scared about what appears to be more violence. It should also be noted that these reports are coming to us over vastly improved, graphic media that scares us even more. What this means is that parents are afraid to let their children run free outside when they get home from school or any other time. (Of course there are parents who are working and leave their children unsupervised when their children get home from school...if they go to school at all. This can lead to the other problems both for the child and for society as a whole.) However with supervised children rerely going outside and spending the majority of their time on computers, I-pads and I-phones, they can end-up socially inept and lonely. Also most children are now drifting even futher away from nature than their parents to have no knowledge or appre-cieation of it at all, They grow up cut off from the Earth, the plants and the animals, which then speeds-up our horrible abuse of the Earth and life's ecosystems. Thus these children getting little or no education about nature in their schools, have no experience of nature, and grow up to continue our spirial into overpopulation and extinction. (To study this in more depth I would reccomend a book called <u>Last Child in the Woods, Saving our Children from Nature-Deficit Disorder</u> by Richard Louv.)

2. Political Chaos

We also take for granted our political systems and believe that they have always existed and always will. However political systems are even more tenuas than family units. Historically political systems are always changing. It is natural for governments to be blamed for all of their nations problems. This is especially true when things start to go wrong from overpopulation. When too many people need too much, many things will be affected...like the rule of law, justice, the courts, the economy, transportation, safety, food and water, and the health and welfare of the people. Though we are in the early stages of this, we can still see it in the instability of nations and governments as they try to circle their wagons to blame other countries and each other for their problems. In frustration, some people single out weak and needful groups to blame for their problems. We have seen that recently all over the world with refugees fleeing for their lives from war, stark poverty and oppression. We forget that governments precariously rest on the wise decision of trusted leaders who seldom exist, the ebb and flow of world markets, the number and size of natural disasters, the keeeping of alliances, the sanity of leaders all over the world, the morality in their agendas, and of course the support of the people. Anything like overpopulation that will alter and upset the evolution of our species, will naturally undermine the political climate to throw the nations of the world into chaos

3. Violence and War

We are already witnessing an increase in the tension between nations. However it will vastly increase as the population grows and our resources shrink to cause violence and war to break out everywhere, At the end of the hunter/gatherer's stage in human evolution, groups of people started coming together to form city-states. However instead of bringing more community and peace, it brought in the evolution of group pride that is leding our species into violence and war. With increasingly large weapons, war, together with the groups that wage them, have become more and more violent to bring on advancing misery and injustice. Recently, through treaties made between nations, people have also come together, which should be good in building peace. However these alliances have meant that an insult or attack of one nation is an insult or attack on all the nations in an alliance. This has resulted in two catastrophic world wars that have brought on shocking destruction, loss of life, and misery. Recently nations have had smaller wars with each other, but the threat of another world war looms constantly over us. Increased population problems will push nations into blame, paranoia and panic that will erupt in confrontations and more wars resulting in violence everywhere..

I believe that overpopulation, which began in the beginning of the 20th century, will progressively contribute to the nations distrust and anger of each other and different cultures. As our population continues to grow, patience and trust will diminish to allow separation and pride to rule everywhere. Eventually people will be fighting for the basic needs of food, water, medical care, sanitation, transportation, safety, and unpolluted land free of flooding. Fish and all marine life will be long gone. I know that some believe that our advanced technology will offer us solutions to all of our problems, including overpopulation and extiction, but from recent experiences, there is no indication that will happen. Thus I would ask, "How can we avoid it, and when will it get started"? There has been no indication that anyone is willing to give up anything that might affect their present lifestyle. We all just continue in the struggle to get more and more money, through more and more "progress" with its growth and prosperity which is growing our population.

Though numerous books have been written on this subject to educate people about what is happening, I see no indication of interest, much less action. Some have said to me, "Why should

I worry about this, because I won't be here?" I find that to be a self- centered, mean, very sad response. It is also a very ignorant response because it ignores the fact that everyone and everything are interconnected. It is also selfish and self-centered because it ignores and throws out all of the people who will follow us...our decendents. It's also very sad because it affirms our lazy, uninformed disinterested state where we are allowing our own species to go extinct.

4. Increasing Prejudice, Ignorance, Selfishness and Greed

I have said that everything in the cosmos is evolving, which means that we are always evolving too. It means that our wisdom, intellect, and morals are also evolving, but are they evolving forward or backward (de-volving)? I have seen some forward evolution in my lifetime, as I have witnessed the advance of justice and equality in my country. I've seen us move toward morality in our acceptance and advancement of women, the poor, handicapped, and people of different cultures, colors, and sexual preference. It has been slow in coming and is far from finished, but there has been some progress. However if we continue to flood the Earth with humans, this evolution of morality will not just be slowed; it will be stopped. War, murder, injustice and abuse are already becoming more accepted. Also as overpopulation continues our swarming the Earth like locusts to wipe out things like fresh water, food, justice, tolerance, peace and world cooperation, we will evolve into monsters with no moral compass and no hope.

For some time the world has seemed to be shrinking because of things like globalization, improved communication, and world trade. It seemed to be helping us to understand each other and stop pre-judging people who are diffent from us. However now we see a new surge in prideful nationalism around the world driven mostly by a fear of terrorists. This has caused us to up the way we prejudge people of other nations, religions, classes, and economic standing to makes us fear and even hate them. We are also moving away from supporting the necessary alliances, and even more, the education that is needed in this complicated world. Now we are allowing ignorance to grow everywhere, even in the highest levels of world governments.

We need to wake up and understand that we are only a tiny part of the interconnected everything, We need to humbly respond to our microscopic place in the endless cosmos. We also need to wisely and humbly come together with kindness, honesty, and love...but we aren't doing that at all! Our morals are de-volving to leave us moving increasingly backward into divisive selfishness and pride. If, as some say, it's true that wisdom is a mixture of knowledge, love and common sense, we are in very big trouble.

It's clear that our overpopulation is a major contributor to this moral deterioration. More people are swarming the planet to eat more food, drink more water, seek more jobs, need more health-care, need more sanitatry conditions, and endless other things. All of this puts pressure on human relationships, law enforcement, governments, and it ups the abuse of our glorious planet. All of this tension and pressure will grow to result in more anger, fear, suspicion and erratic behavior. We will progressively treat each other harshly and cruely to erode our morality and tear apart any form of community. Needless to say, we will find our lives to be increasingly hard and ugly. We will rebel, in our helplessness, bitterness, hopelessness and lawlessness, to where survival of the fittest, rather than reflective morality, will become our only moral compuss. We will have become a deviate, destructive species in the cosmos that cannot possibly survive,

C. Increasing Land, Water and Air Pollution

Even though we have addressed this before, I will approch it again because it bares repeating. Becsause we have people swarming the Earth like proverbial locusts, our pollution is appauling. It is obvious that we have never been the cleanest of animals, but what we are doing now is riduculous. Also individual humans have always polluted their living space, but it happened at a time when human population was low. At that time, the Earth was able to clean up our mess. However now, because of our massive numbers, our pollution has become massive to a point where the Earth cannot possibly handle it. We also know from our studies on the evolution of life that when a species runs afoul of its ecosystem, it is soon gone, It becomes necessary for the Eaarth to replace it and move on. In the same way, we will soon be gone. Just look at it!

We are polluting the **air** with our automobiles, airplanes, coal power plants, nuclear tests, endless particles, and more. We see it in health reports that reveal our rising asthma, lung-cancer, emphysema, and many other diseases. We see it in the accumulation of Co2 in the atmosphere to create the green house effect. It causes vastly raising sea levels, the redirecting the the streams of the oceans, the changing of the ecosystems and their plant growth, the production of bigger and bigger storms and wildfires, and the melting the ice of arctic regions and glacers. It is heating up our planet to change the temperature of everything including ourselves, and the rising heat of the air is helping to eliminate the essential plant life on the Earth that produces the oxygen that we must have to live.

We are also polluting our **waters** with chemicals like fertilizers, oil from ships, boats and oil-leaks, run-off from roads, the flooding in vast areas that fill everything with junk, and all of our endless trash and plastic accumulation. We are also destroying the water ecosystems with things like like dams and sewage plants. We have killed off the "stream buffers", which are the vegetation around areas of water that filter them. Different areas of the world have started fighting with each other over their present and future sources of fresh water. Also, with global warming, we are increasingly melting away the glaciers that have been our chief fresh water reserves that have served us and all of the animals on the Earth. Many scientists believe that the availability of fresh water will be our first critical problem as we move closer to extinction. We can't count on removing the salt from ocean water to serve our drinking needs because the oceans themselves are becoming toxic. They too are in trouble because of pavement run-off, dangerous plastic invasions, nuclear waste leaks, and fishing tackle, net, and trash dumping. Thus we are wiping out marine life that some say will come in just twenty years.

Our pollution and abuse of the Earth's **land** is often given the least amount of thought, but actually it is the most dangerous of all. It's not just that we don't recognize the value of the land;

it's that we don't seem to care about the land at all! We have no recognition, feeling or concern about it because we seldom ever think about it. When we do, we see the land as being something that is endless, and something that is ours. This can be seen in such things as the way we draw lines on maps to mark off areas of the Earth that each of us then claim to own. We think we can do anything we want with it...and what we do is not good. Without hesitation, we eliminate the lands vegetation to build big personal houses, offices, places of worship, sport centers, government buildings, schools, skyscrapers, and more. We endlessly pave over the land for roads and parking lots. We poison the land with chemicals and dig and blow it up to get things like coal. When we naturally do these things, we are taking part in our ultimate pollution of the Earth. It's the most dangerous because in so many ways, we live on, and live off, of the land.

All of this pollution and much more is now killing more people than wars, hunger, automobiles, aids, malaria, storms or anything else. However please don't say even in jest, that such a cruel reality might be good for controlling the population. I have even heard it flippantly said that what we need are more wars to reduce the population. Such cruel, prideful, ignorant statements only point out the reason we are in this mess. It indicates how people don't care about each other or for those who will follow us because they are so lost in pride and greed that they don't care about anything but themselves.

D. Increasing Loss of Animals and Plants

Obviously as pollution grows with overpopulation, even more plants and animals will be lost. However there is more behind it than that, because there is a huge thing that may even outweighs our pollution. It is that we have lost our sense of being one with, and connected to, the plants and animals and the Earth. We don't see them as fellow voyagers in the evolution on this planet as our ancestors instinctively knew. They revered the plants and animals, and at times they even worshiped them. They would honor them in their ceremonies and offer them thanks for sacrificing their lives so our ancestors could live on. We have not only lost all of that, but we have come to disregard and abuse them and ignore the fact that they have lives at all.

We see *animals* as being enemies that we need to fear and fight. We turn them into our slaves and abuse them. We even kill them mercilessly for sport (which I think is cruel and insane). We also see *plants* as being lifeless, meaningless hindrances to our building, paving, sports venues or anything else that makes money. In our farming, we cruelly manipulate them (as we do with our pets) to grow bigger, smaller, without seeds, or anything else that makes more money. Also as we do with animals, we use degrading chemicals to make them grow bigger. In other words the main reason why animals, trees and shrubs are being wiped out so quickly is because we just don't care. We put money to buy more and more meaningless things over life. We want money, progress and other things, and if that is at the expense of plants and animals, we don't care!

Of course the equally insane part of this is that we need them. We need them to survive. Everything we eat comes either from an animal or some kind of plant. Since that is true, how can we not care about them? How can we not encourage and care for them instead of wiping them out through our overpopulation, rampant pollution, destruction of their habitat, and our cruelty, abuse and disregard? It's crazy, because we need them so much! Of course it's also true that they need us. They need us to not abuse and destroy them, but they also need us to love, assist and nurture them as our siblings in the Earth's evolution.

Overpopulation is the great supercharger of all our insane actions so it's become a driving force. As we now need more and more meat and vegetables to feed the masses, we actually have far less. As we progressively wipe out animals, forests, and available farm land, we wipe out any chance of our species surviving. As we don't care about plants and animals, the Earth will not care about us. The Earth cannot allow a disconnected, destructive, mean species to destroy everything.

E. The Destruction of the Earth's Ecosystems

An Ecosystems is a biological community or environment of a complex network of interconnected systems that sustains life on the Earth. Often people speak of "The" ecosystem, as if there were just one. I suppose it might be argued that in some way the whole Earth forms an ecosystem, but even though the Earth is an interconnected planet, using the word ecosystem as we define it, is not true . When we talk about ecosystems, we're talking about how the evolution of life on the outer layer of the Earth functions and continues to exist. This outer layer is made up of many different ecosystems that sustain life in many different ways. This means that all life forms live within, and are a functioning part, of one, and probably several, ecosystems.

The question of the number of the ecosystems on the Earth is impossible for us to know because each one of them is unique, interconnected and very complex. Thus to try to count them makes no sense. For instance there are unique ecosystems in every mud-puddle, pile of dirt, sand, snow or leaves, and of course in all of various depths of the ocean and rising mountains. Each animal and plant, as well as each one of us, is a unique ecosystem. For instance, we can witness that in us when we see different people contracting different diseases or being affected by different foods, drugs, or bug-bites. Obviously the most complex, interconnected ecosystems of all are "brains", Still being the organizing but simplistic beings that we are, we try to put the major ecosystems into easy categorys. One example of this might be:

a. Aquatic ecosystems

Marine

Fresh Water

   Terrestrial Ecosystems

Forest

Littoral Zone

Kiparian Zone

   Sub-surface Lithoautotropic Ecosystems

Microbale

Urbane

Desert

b. Another simpler categorization would be:

Forest Ecosystems

Grassland Ecosystems

Desert Ecosystems

Tundra Ecosystems

Freshwater Ecosystems

Marine Ecosystems

Of course any attempt to tie down an evolution like ecosystems is ridiculous. Like the Earth itself, the balanced, complex ecosystems will always remain a mystery to us. However there is one thing about them that cannot be denied. As reflective mammals living on this Earth, we can witness the *needed balance* of plants and animals that allows humans to survive, and how they provide us with sustenance like food and water, Obviously we should always cherish all of the Earth's ecosystems, and never bother or destroy them! At an early age, we should be taught (by our parents and our schools) that ecosystems are basic to our life and all life, and that when we hurt them, we are hurting ourselves. However this is not being taught to either children or adults, so most people know noth-ing about them. This leaves us, in our ignorance, destroying them all the time...and when we obliterate them, we are on the way out.

Overpopulation is a part of this foolishness because it is constantly adding to and multiplying our numbers, which adds to and multiplies the death of the ecosystems. For instance, the more people tear down trees to build houses; the more they rape the land to do away with the oxygen we need from the plants. All of our selfish commercial altering of the Earth attacks the delicate layer of the ecosystems that makes up the Earth's life forms. Soon in our ignorance, pride and greed, the balance of the ecosystems will be so abused, sick and destroyed that we will no longer exist. *We* will be gone, but the *Earth* will go on to resuscitate its ecosystems to allow life to once again blossom abundantly. We will be gone, but the Earth will evolve on its way into the endless cosmos.

F. Unavailable Drinking Water and Food

This may sound like something that is simple and obvious, but it's not! That's because we simply *do not believe* that there could possibly be a time when the Earth's drinking water and food would not be there. Of course today some people in war-torn areas, or after some natural catastrophes, have felt this sick agony, but most people blindly assume that food and drinking water will always be there. However many scientists today are saying that we are not that far away from facing this basic and frightening reality, and overpopulation is mainly responsible.

We all agree that it would be horrible if people started dying off in large numbers from a lack of the two basic things that humans need to live. However if you look around, you can see that this is already happening all over the world. If we don't address our overpopulation, it will be happening all the time, everywhere. If we can take seriously that we need drinking water and it is not something we can take-for-granted, and if we can realize that overpopulation is doing things like encouraging climate change to melt ice sheets that have provided fresh water preserves, and the pollution that is destroying the Earth's rivers and oceans...perhaps then we can wake-up, change and start to depopulate. Perhaps we can turn-around and preserve fresh water and food for the future. If we can realize that the same overpopulation that is pushing us to kill off the trees and shrubbery of the Earth, is taking out the viable farm land that is increasingly hard to find. Also if we can reverse our slaughter of the ecosystems to allow animals to live right beside us, to declare a peace where we can assist each other...yes, if we can come out of our prideful ignorance enough to depopulate and be a decent, real part of our mother Earth, perhaps there will be enough food and water to sustain us for for the years ahead.

That is a lot of "ifs", and I fear there are far too many "ifs" and not enough that "is" actually being done. This leaves us going over the cliff of extinction...and we don't care. What can *I* do? What can *we* do? We're all slightly different, so we all must answer that for ourselves, but one thing is sure; we all have to do something now!

G. Constant Violence and War

As drinking water and food get scarce from overpopulation; there will be a huge growth in fear, anger, and violence. When any species is fighting for its life, it gets ugly. We are no exception. Distrust, violence and war becomes the norm. We can already see this happening as we witness our cruel bombing in meaningless wars that sends desperate refugees running for their lives to seek refuge in other countries, who then cause paranoia, abuse and cruelty as we refuse to help them. This is fueled by growing sick prejudices, with their mean lies, that grow out of the increasingly crazy fears that have taken us over.

Of course, as the world's population continues to rise, all of these things will get worse. We will soon reach a point where no nation or group of people is able to trust another. Everyone will be fighting for their survival searching for things like drinking water, food, and a safe place to sleep. All past relationships, treaties, agreements, avenues of communication between nations, as well as personal relationships, laws, morality and individual interactions, will be wiped out. Years of dysfunction in collapsing nations will leave our species lost, alone and insane. Finally chaos like we cannot imagine will come to the few survivors who are left buried in thirst, starvation and disease. It will result in a mercifull end to their existence. Our prideful, ignored over-population will have led to no population at all, because when something could have been done about it, nothing was.

If this sounds like a horror movie or a bad dream, you are partially correct. It is certainly horrible, but it is vastly different from a movie or a dream. It is far from having the silly, imagined horror plot that movies turn out for our entertainment, and this is certainty no dream. What we are talking about here is the projection of scientific facts that are presently accepted and can be observed all around us, and that is not entertaining! This is talking about what will happen to our children's children or their relatives...to those who follow us. It is already happening to the plants and animals that we haven't already destroyed. (They are our relatives too, but we've avoided and discarded that fact.) When I think about it, there is no word that can describe all of this, because it's so much worse than any tragedy, disaster, catastrophe, war or anything else that we have ever experienced or imagined. It is not something we can picture or identify, so we respond to it with denial or escape it or anger. You see, overpopulation's results are not just bringing about the end of a person's life, the results are bringing about the end of every person's life on this planet...forever!

H. An Increase in Global Warming

I have saved this one to the last because it is also a very serious problem. However in spite of ignorant resistance, it is at least being addressed. Nations have come together to discuss it and hear the scientific reports that help them understand its repercussions. However little is being done about it, so it continues to grow, and it's obvious that everyday that our population grows, global warming gets worse.

My wife and I were trained to teach about this throughout North Carolina, and we did that for three years. We taught people how global warming has positively been proven through numerous scientific studies. We showed them how the high presence of carbon dioxide in the atmosphere in past times had caused the Earth to warm because of the green-house effect. The great analogy for this is how a car can heat up to dangerous levels in the sun when the windows are closed. Every year we witness the tragic deaths of children left in cars where the windows were up. This same thing is now happening to us in global warming as carbon dioxide lets the heat of the sun in, but then blocks it from going out. This has happened before to alter the weather patterns of the Earth, but this time is different. This time *we are doing it.* It's not being caused as it was before by a natural disaster, such as a meteor strike or a huge volcanic uprising. No now it is being caused by the carbon dioxide released into the atmosphere in recent years from things like factories, automobiles, airplanes, and, most of all, power-companies that use coal to produce energy. Unless this can be stopped, it will not destroy the Earth or totally bring about our extinction, but it will cause our species incredible grief as oceans rise to wipe out the islands and large cities around the coasts. Also storms will grow and the ecosystems will change to kill off countless plants and animals. In other words, it will be a mess, and overpopulation is now feeding it so it will come more quickly and be much worse!

I. Extinction

Yes, extinction really is going to happen (just as our overpopulation of the Earth has happened in the just 100 years). Extinction is where we are now headed. and it cannot be denied by any informed, aware person who has not been brainwashed by pride and greed's dance. Money is important to our economic systems, and the growth of the population feeds those economic systems, but isn't the fact that we are *looking extinction in the eye* is a little more important? Shouldn't the survival of our species, and the existence of our future ancestors, cause us to find a way to limit the number of people being born to couples to just one or less children?

The good news, that we will talk more about in the next section, is that if we can limit the number of children being born to couples, it will mean that in just a few generations the problem will be solved. We will have reached a sustainable number that the Earth can tolerate (something around seven hundred and fifty million). Then this miraculous planet could heal itself from most of our selfish abuses. The animals and plants could return, the rivers, lakes, streams and oceans could clear themselves of our pollution, and the numerous ecosystems of the Earth could naturally balance themselves to allow all life-forms to live and blossom.

Of course even though this may sound simple and encouraging, it's not. I'll bet you don't know anybody right now who believes that we could reach a point where everybody would only have one child. One of the main reasons is that we are all tied to preserving this culture of advancing wealth and what we call progress (which only really helps the wealthy). However, the rich always manage to keep the poor believing that this money culture is also helping them. Thus what we call "progress" will be a huge block to ever addressing, or doing any thing about, overpopulation. There are many other things that will make it hard for us to make the changes necessary to end our overpopulation, but we will discuss them later.

V.

WHAT WILL HAPPEN IF WE DO ADDRESS OVERPOPULATION?

Nothing good can come out of ignoring overpopulation. However if we recognize it, and then try to do something about it, there will be some obvious positive species-saving results, but there will also be problems with negative reactions. It will set in motion some demanding, hard-to-solve and challenging problems. Therefore, since I am trying to seek the truth here, I will honestly address the demands of doing something, along with the huge advantages. Of course I must repeat that I believe that the problems, that will come from our addressing this reality are nothing to what will happen if we don't! I grieve that most people presently refuse to even think about or learn about it, much less rationally address it. I have observed this is because it's just too threatening. It frightens us and is too complicated. so most people refuse to take it in. I am trying to sound the alarm in this book to shake us out of this apathy that is leading our species into misery and quicker extinction. Here are the hard negatives and positives of what will happen if we ever do address overpopulation.

A. Negative Results

Strong Resistance From Both Women and Men

There is no question that trying to just honestly address overpopulation will cause both women and men to be extremely upset. Most of them will see their lives tied to having children. Also it was not that long ago that having a lot of children was the expected norm. Men would often identify their worth as being the bread-winner for their family and children, and women would identify themselves as child-bearers In most cases, none of this has really changed. even though some women have moved beyond it. However in most areas of the world, women still feel that their purpose in life is to have children.

Many **men** see having children as being connected to their ego and being macho. For many men, having children may not necessarily involve being married. I recently heard a man ask another, "Do you have any children". He replied, "None that I know of," and strutted off. To have children for many men is to be manly. They certainty don't want that tampered with. Many times I have heard of wealthy men having numerous children, so in some ways, having children may also be seen as a sign of success.

All of this means that if you start telling men something that might threaten them having children, they will feel personally insulted and feel that their egos are being threatened. In other words, just mentioning overpopulation and its possible corrections will make some men very angry. People don't want to talk about or face this subject and will do anything to avoid it. Several times when I was talking about this to a group, a man would get up and walk out.

We are an escapist society, and many think that men try to escape more than women. There are many reasons for this, but I think the fact that women carry their babies and then care for them, makes them more honest about the reality around them. Women have traditionally been called the "culture bearers", while men have been called the "hunters". It seems to me that culture bearers rather than hunters might be the ones that are more in touch with reality, However the fact is that the subject of overpopulation is not popular with either men or women.

The reason **women** feel threatened is that there really does seem to be something called a "maternal instinct". Women have carried children for so long in our species' evolution that it has become a part of their inherited consciousness. Many women have said to me that they feel a real need to have another baby. It seems that when they have one that, even after the anguish of giving birth, they instinctively want another. Of course whether they actually do this usually depends on a number of things. Economics, political upheaval, an acceptable and willing man, mental and physical health, and many other considerations can go into women actually having another baby...but I think that the instinctive pull is still there. This may mean that bringing up the subject of overpopulation, and what is needed to correct it, will be even less popular with women than it is with men. Just as I have had men leave when I talked about it, I have also had some women leave.

It is true that women are being increasingly accepted in the work-place, have the availability of many birth-controls, and benefit from the many inventions for what has been called "women's work" so they can do other things. Also with more and more people living together before marriage and getting married later, fewer women are now choosing to have children. World population growth has dropped from the incredible expanse of the twentieth century in the last few years because of numerous factors. However it will still rise to nine billion at around 2040, so this slight drop in births offers no real encouragement. As I've said, some people are using this statistic to say that there is no problem even though we are already seven billion over a sustainable limit. These minor drops are just natural adjustment to change and will not in any way alter the wrath of women if we try to do anything about overpopulation.

We need to face it: Both men and women will resist anything that would alter or limit them having children. For them, the only solution is for us to ignore it. It could be argued that this one negative reality that is enough to stop this discussion, will assure our species' extinction.

Resistance from Religions, Conservatives and Society

Some **religions** see marriage as being strictly for the purpose of having children, They think that's what marriage is all about. I have seen priests pray for the fertility of the woman in her marriage ceremony. Also many religions think birth-control is a sin, and they do everything they can to discourage it. They believe that for everyone the more children they can have the better. Many of the world's religions have scriptures that say things like "be fruitful and multiply" which encourages unlimited children and more overpopulation. Of course there are indications that religions are making some adjustments on the way they approach marriage and birth control, but there is still a long way to go. As for now, religion's acceptance of unlimited children is a huge block to any discussion or change in our overpopulation of the Earth.

There have always been people who have resisted change. They have often been labeled **conservatives**. They are often not very interested in the needy but in protecting military and recovering the past. Of course there are always people who embrace change, are concerned for the needy, work for peace and justice rather than militarism, and feel directed toward the future. In the past these two groups have held different opinions, but they were still able to respect and work with each other both in and outside of governments. However recently, the world seems to have polarized into strong conservative and liberal groups to elicit anger and distrust to the detriment of everybody. In addition, the world is now being torn apart by religious extremists who feel that the nations of the West have abused them. Ill-advised bombings have brought forth radical terrorists acts of violence that are causing the Western nations to become even more conservative, exclusive and divisive. Conservatives have always been suspicious of any talk about overpopulation, but within this environment, they will be even more hostile. There is no doubt that just as religions have trouble accepting the fact of overpopulation, the conservatives of today will respond with even more negativity.

Societies and cultures of the word have evolved over time to keep local traditions and meet the needs of the people. They often evolve with strong, dictatorial leaders, however many have recently begun to accept the advantages of democracy. Also economies have evolved to first use a system of exchange, but it has now evolved into a complicated money exchange. Today we have evolved a new economic system based on new evolving technologies. The societies of the world are being confused, stressed, tested, and challenged by these changes, It cannot be denied that the subject of overpopulation will just deposit another big, demanding stress into this mix so that most of the world's societies will be slow in their acceptance. They will try everything to block out its demands. We are now so bogged down in the divisions and struggles that come out of national and religious pride, with its violence and wars, that we will feel that we can't handle or be stressed further by anything else.

Resistance to Change in:

a. **Sex and Marriage**

The urge to reproduce is found in every life form. It's the major thing that keeps a species from going extinct. In early life forms, this was done just by those of the same species moving from being one as they broke apart and became two. All evolution in the cosmos moves forward as particles come together to form something new, so its natural that in the same way, the species of the Earth have evolved to merge together to form something new. The life forms on the Earth began to feel strong urges to unite with another. These urges allowed each of its species to have a variety of genes that helped them to evolve and survive. Higher life forms like plants have evolved ingenious and imaginative ways to pollinate, even using other beings, to survive. They've even used the wind and animals like bees, to take their pollen to other plants. Of course in animals, there is a strong urge to reproduce by a male putting his semen into a female.

We humans are no different because we too have very strong urges. Males feel a strong urge to do this, and of course a woman has similar urges to receive it. Many, like Sigmund Freud, have said that this basic urge in us is so strong that it can rule our lives. Though many may find this to be an exaggeration, it cannot be denied that men are usually conscious of being macho to attract women, and women tend to be conscious of being sexy to attract men. The practice of men fighting over and violently sexually taking women has evolved out, but there are still far too many problems of men sexually abusing women. It would be a great day if we could have a rise in the value of, and compassion for, both women and children. We still have a long way to go.

Marriage emerged as a way for both parents to take care of their children and a way to encourage men to take care of women as they raised children. Marriage has now evolved to be a sacred institution in religions, and it is accepted in almost all cultures. However it has been acted out in different ways. As I said, marriage is often seen as the only place that children can be raised, and marriage is seen as existing to have children. Thus women at a certain age are expected and pressured to marry, but the way that this happens varies. In some religions or cultures the parents choose the mate, while in others they hire someone to do it. Recently with the rise of romantic love, the husband and wife are supposed to choose each other.

Some people are already curbing having children for mostly economic reasons. However when the call comes for this is to be done to reverse population growth, it will still be resisted. That's because both sex and marriage in their traditional forms do not easily adapt to change, and to reverse population would certainly require powerful changes.

b. **The Concept of Family**

Families began as men and women bonded to raise children. Thus the traditional picture of a family is a man, woman, and two or more children. As with sex and marriage, this picture of a family has been seen as sacred. However, in spite of this, the interpretation of a family has recently begun to change. It has been brought on by household inventions that have helped women to clean the houses and cook the food. This, and the First World War, led women to start working beside men, and that led to an increase in the equality of women. Underlying all of this was the invention of various birth control methods that allowed women and men to decide when they would have children.

Thus most families have fewer children than they would have had before, but the still continuing growth in population has kept that from being any help to the environment. Also amazing advancements in medicine now have people living at least twice as long as they did before which has vastly grown the population and even helped to change what the word family means. Very recently, the horrible prejudices against same sex people has been dropping enough to allow them to marry and adopt children.

All of this means that the old picture of families has already changed. However if we take overpopulation seriously and decide to limit the children in families to one or none, it will mean another huge change to the meaning of family. Traditionalists will cry out against it as an insult to "family values".

c. **Laws and Governments**

Laws and governments are based around the evolved morality of their constituents. We like to think that laws bring about justice, but that's not always true. For instance there were recently laws supporting slavery and opposing women's rights, civil rights, and marriage rights. Actually there have been laws throughout history that have tried to halt the moral evolution of our species. Some laws have even been ridiculous. There was a law in my home-town when I was growing up that said no automobiles were allowed downtown because they frightened the horses. Of course that was not enforced and was soon just forgotten, but this certainly makes the point that laws are not infallible and can certainly be wrong. Still many people think that way, and resist changing any laws.

To stop overpopulation, laws will need to be passed that will not be well received. It will not be easy to get people to face, listen to, read or understand why we have to make changes to stop over-population, but it will be even harder to get laws passed to facilitate it. Governments must first be convinced to come together and stand up for the elimination of overpopulation's disaster. They must understand and be convinced that if we don't do something, our species will soon be extinct. They must also see what it is doing to the Earth and its plants and animals. Only with the education of most of the people on the Earth, in order to understand and do something about this, will any laws be passed...and we are far from being there!

d. **Views on Economics, Progress and Money**

These next two negative things are the worst. I've mentioned before that most of the cultures in the world are based on them, and if overpopulation is to be addressed at all, there will have to be some changes in these assumptions. Progress and making money have evolved to be embedded in our economic systems and to question them in any way has become unthinkable. Most of the jobs that have come after the industrial revolution are directly tied to money and progress. To say, "making any suggestion to change this would not be well received" doesn't begin to describe what would happen when suggestions are made to stop overpopulation..

For instance I am aware that the rich people of world almost own everything. Thus they are seen as the ones who give people jobs that ordinary people must have to survive. Thus our whole economic system is built around the wealthy getting wealthier through growth and progress (which means more and more people needing more and more things). Unless this monetary growth and progress mania can be addressed and changed, nothing can ever be done about overpopulation. To have one child will dramatically effect the number of people who buy things, so commercially it is a negative. Also fewer youth in the work-place to take jobs and provide money to sustain the elderly will dramatically lessen progress, and it will certainly make rich people mad. However some people say that when it becomes obvious that we have to choose between finding another way to run our economy or *going extinct*, we will ultimately find a way to adjust our economy...but, will we? Also, of course, if we wait too long, it will be too late, because we'll be gone.

e. **The Perceived Assault on Individual Rights**

I have observed that this subject comes up every time the subject of any population control comes up. It is obvious that the only way that births will be slowed is through some type of community, national or world effort to limit the number of births, and that is often interpreted as a limitation of individual rights. There is no question that the rights of individuals to make their own decisions are important in some circumstances, but not in all. That's why we have laws. Laws limit the right of individuals to do certain thing. There are laws about how an individual can drive a car, a boat, an airplane and many more. We limit the time that individually-run businesses can close, and even how they can be run. We have laws of all kinds that keep individuals from hurting others. We could go on with this, but the point is that sometimes the rights of the whole outweigh the rights of the few. The delicate balance between individual and collective rights is something that will always be debated. It is often decided in the courts, but it can also rest on things like common sense, justice, compassion and long-term thinking.

We have seen this same argument in the discussion of guns being made available to the public. The advantages of only allowing guns to be used by the military have been proven both with statistics and the results from the gun-free nations that have tried it. However the fact that thousands and thousands of lives have been saved in those countries has been ignored. The arguments for guns for the public has always been based on individual rights. (They also claim that the right for everyone to bear arms is actually in the U.S. constitution.) Nobody likes to be told what to do, although parents, laws and rules do that everyday. However history shows that the people of the nations who opposed gun control when their nations first voted to do so, changed their minds soon after their nation became gun free. The dramatic drop in crime and deaths in countries that have banned guns often soon means that it has the full support of the people. They see that many lives have been saved, and they realize that what they've given up is nothing compared to what they've gained in human lives. The original arguments about abused individual rights are replaced by the public's right to live...and live safely.

We must find a way to make this same thing happen in regard to overpopulation. We must ask people if their individual right to have many children is more important than our collective right to exist on this planet? We must ask if our selfish individual rights are more important than our species going extinct through an unimaginably horrible process (involving things like violence, war, starvation, thirst and sickness)? Is the right to continue to have many children that further contribute to overpopulation, worth condemning the relatives who will follow us to the despicable suffering that will come in the process of our species going extinct? Would this selfish, naive decision to do nothing because of individual rights, really be worth it? We have to find a way for people to get out of this prideful, self-centered mindset and look beyond just themselves to actually take-in *what we're doing and where we're going.*

We are suppose to be an intelligent species but our pride and greed keep wiping that out. Certainly we are wiping-out how we are destroying the ecosystems that support us as our numbers grow beyond insane! Still we have a little time left to wake up. Perhaps our intelligent, rational buried selves will kick in soon. Perhaps overpopulation, that is now totally discarded by almost everyone, will somehow be brought forward enough to be heard, understood and accepted so that some action can be taken. However the present vacuum of logic and comprehension does not bode well for future actions.

B. Positive Results

Obviously I believe that the positive results of addressing this issue far outweigh the negatives ones. To me, it's a no-brainier because it has to do with *survival over extinction.* I will try to list a few of the positive results, but it would be impossible to list them all. There is no possible way that anyone could know all of them, and even if they did, this book could never hold them. Also remember that at this point in human evolution, we are really messed up. Awash in our prideful, greedy thoughts and actions, it is hard to look out and see the truth about much of anything. Still as a person who is struggling to see a way forward, I will now list some positive things that I believe will happen if we do address overpopulation.

1. Less Crowding and improved relationships

The first of these is obvious. As our population drops, the *over-crowding* of cities, where people come to get employment, will drop. Horrible traffic *conditions* will progressively decrease, which means that fewer people will be maimed or die from car and truck accidents. *Living conditions* will also be improved by having more space, trees, shrubs, and a clear blue sky. As time goes by, people will *discover nature* again. They will see how beautiful it is and that it is not an enemy to be conquered but a friend to love, enjoy and be cared for. They will learn again that having space to live and enjoy nature brings peace and regeneration, but seeing nature as a thing that is our enemy to be ignored and used can only bring pain, division and death.

They will also discover that not just other humans can be their friends and companions, but all of the *plants and animals* can offer community as well. They will rediscover and come home to their amazing, *warm connectedness to the Earth and its many life-forms*. They will come to see that fighting the Earth and its many life-forms, and fighting other people (as we live out pride's divisive teachings) is not only unnecessary, but is destroying us.. In other words, they will finally find the way to the peace for which they have so long been searching.

2. Less Self-centered Negativity, Violence and War

I have already spoken about how crowded conditions cause anger, frustration, and even fighting. Thus one of the main advantages to less crowded conditions is bound to be a more relaxed and fulfilling association with other people around us. This would provide *less violence, crime, even an end to war*. It might allow nations and cultures to elicit trust rather than fear and cooperation instead of confrontation. It might also mean that with the internet, most jobs would be found outside of a single office-space in towns and cities allowing people to work as they spread out to enjoy the wonders of nature. Most of us have grown accustomed and adjusted to overcrowded conditions. This means that many people now enthusiastically defend it. Most of us can't comprehend living in any other way because overcrowded conditions are all we know. Of course we will admit that our hectic, run-around lives immersed in massive traffic jams and car exhaust is neither healthy nor pleasant. We may even sometime think that there might be a better way to live, and retire to the country.

We have evolved to be a prideful, self-centered species that has almost lost its miracle of reflectivity. Instead of recognizing, and affirming, our connectedness to everything, we are pridefully labelling everything but ourselves as irrelevant and even bad. Our continued uninformed, insensitive overpopulation attests to the fact that we are ignoring everything around us (like the Earth, the plants, the animals, and the ecosystems), to focus on nothing but ourselves.

It stands to reason that if we could come out of our self-centeredness enough, we would be able to actually face our overpopulation,. It would also allow us to see each other and other species as being just as alive, miraculous, and precious as ourselves. The horrible negativity, in which pride has immersed us, is drowning us. We're afraid of everything because we see everything but ourselves as being threatening and bad. This will depart when we humbly accept who we really are and break-out of ourselves to rationally address our overpopulation.

I believe that our reflective state means that deep down we are still aware of what pride is doing to us. Also deep down we know what overpopulation is doing to us. There is no question that our prideful, negative approach to everything is eating away our soul. I have found that joy is seldom found in our species. Only the shallow releases of our false escapes ever cheer us. Addressing overpopulation would be a big step out of the negative chains in which pride has enslaved us.

3. Coming together to find humility, peace and community

In my second book I talked about how the cosmos advances as everything comes together to be more complex than it was before. However we have chosen separating pride over uniting humility, love, kindness, peace, and all the other things that bring us together. It seems obvious to me that if we can face the obvious fact that all Homo sapiens on this planet really are going extinct, and this despicable overpopulation is in the middle of it, we too will come together to also be something more than we were before. It could even mean that we might live real, connected lives of peace on this amazing planet that birthed us.

We might rediscover the things that pride has taken from us. We might learn to love everyone everywhere, as well as the Earth and all of its species. We might rediscover our natural humility, to be able to sympathize and really care for other people, plants and animals. We might rediscover what kindness, sharing, forgiveness, peace and justice really mean. We might learn to be who we as reflective beings are supposed to be, as we use our reflective powers to further the advancement of everything instead of just ourselves. In other words...we might learn to be real!

4. Gradually Rebuilding the Ecosystems

We are now destroying the ecosystems, but if we can stop our overpopulation, it would naturally help to rebuild them. Of course this sounds like speeding down the road and making a U-turn to go back the other way, because right now, nobody even wants to know about it. However I do think that if we can open our eyes and realize what we've done, it could happen. However we still have a long way to go before we will be able to recognize, understand, and stop destroying the ecosystems.

We would need to reach out and teach everyone. We would need to teach them first that there really is such a thing as ecosystems, and then show them how important they are to us and all life on the Earth, We could start by teaching everyone that ecosystems are on the upper level of the Earth where most life exists, and that it is the balance of them that allows all life to continue. Ecosystems feed off of this balance since they are made of numerous life-forms who feed off of each other. When even one life-form in an ecosystem disappears, the health of the whole system becomes affected, and when many life-forms are gone, the ecosystem dies out.

Right now we are dramatically harming the Earth's ecosystems by killing-off a large part of the Earth's vegetation and over fifty per-cent of its animals. This has put all of the Earth's ecosystems in serious jeopardy, as we blindly drift into a place that the

Earth cannot tolerate. We are clearly one of the Earth's evolutions gone bad, so it will dispose of us as it must do to keep life going on it's surface. We will be gone, but the Earth will go on to heal itself and build back its wounded, assaulted ecosystems so that the evolution of life on its surface can continue. (The Earth is not "alive" in the same way that we are, but I do believe that it, and everything else in the cosmos, have various degrees of consciousness...and the Earth has an abundance)

However if we do address, and start doing something about, our overpopulation, we will be beginning to rebuild the ecosystems, so we can gradually dispose of our suicidal foolishness. Clearly the lower the population becomes, the quicker the ecosystems will balance themselves and the better off all life-forms will be. Nature (meaning what is natural) will rebound to allow us to build real, humble, compassionate lives on this amazing Earth we will come to respect and love again.

5. Having a Real Future in the Cosmos

The lives we live now are not built on reality. They are based on angry, self-centered, cruel and sick lies. We feel we must have more money while other people starve. We feel we must be better than everyone else because we think we deserve it. We feel we have to control everything and every body because we are "the best". We *turn a blind eye* to a lot of things like: young men dying in stupid wars out of our religious or national pride and our cruel treatment of the land and plants. We slaughter animals in cruel, industrialized farming. We ignore the world's injustices that don't affect "me", and especially those that may make me richer. We put up with prejudices against women, minorities, the disabled, refugees, same sex oriented people, the sick, the old, the mentally impaired and many more. Now we are turning a blind eye to over-population as people ignore the evidence and insist that there is no problem...and if there is a problem, their god will take care of it, or it will go away on its own. Most of us even believe that couples should have more and more children to bring "progress', and we look down on those who purposely choose not to have children as being selfish and irresponsible because they are not doing what they were made to do, or what there religion tells them do.

The truth is that we are connected to everybody and every-thing, which means we *are* everything and everybody. We live as a part of, and are equal to, everything. Our overpopulation is an insult to this truth. It is making a fool of us. It is unthinkable not to stop something that is destroying the interconnected plants and animals around us when we know how to stop it! It is clear that we are the ones doing it, and we know how we can stop overpopula-tion. However to do it would upset our selfish, cruel, disconnected cultures and life styles. Rich people, companies, individuals and nations might not be able to have more and more money than they need, so they can get bigger and richer to wage more wars. To ignore and do nothing about overpopulation with its insane results is one of pride's most disgusting results. It is driven by our self-centered myths of disconnectedness.

If we can just see that overpopulation is real, and that it is even now affecting us, and if we can see that it is already destroying some of the life on this Earth, we can then move on to correct it and stand tall before the cosmos once again. We will have begun to live in truth, hope and security rather than in the disconnecting lies of pride that leave us in constant fear of each other and the promise of extinction. We will be able to once more anticipate a real and positive future in the cosmos rather than a dark and hopeless one. We will have begun to evolve, as any reflective species should, into being a contributor to the earth's great evolution. We will have begun to be real and come home to who we really are.

VI.

THE ONLY REAL SOLUTION!

A. Reviewing the Causes of Overpopulation

We now know that overpopulation is caused by several things, but first we have to admit that **it is caused by us!** We are the ones overpopulating. No other species on the Earth is involved in any way. Of course looking at us, we can see that it›s caused by our stupidity, greed, and apathy as we have evolved to see the Earth and its life-forms as being of no real value or importance. Some have said that overpopulation is also caused by women's maternal instincts which demand more and more children and also by men's constant lust. Others blame religions, competitiveness or a lack of education. However whatever the cause, we know that it means that all of us have covered the Earth with billions of people without any thought of what it's doing to the ecosystems of the Earth or its plants and animals. Today everyone *should have already* become aware of this, but they aren't and that fact is the major cause of our overpopulation. Human ignorance and selfishness, underlined by all the silly escapes we live in, are propelling our overpopulation over the top. However even if we were to accept overpopulation and try to alter it, we still would have a hard time doing anything. Also time is running out and we can't change this overnight.

It is obvious that **medical advances,** such as vaccinations, the discovery of germs, antibiotics and many other things have dramatically improved treatment in hospitals to cause the population to grow as people continue to get older and older. People now live over twice as long as they did one hundred years ago which has not only driven up the population, it has also complicated health care for everyone and especially for the elderly. Even though wars have escalated the ways they kill people, and ever new viruses and diseases are appearing, they have done nothing to slow overpopulation. People have said to me in jest, "Maybe some nation should drop the hydrogen bomb", or "maybe we should have more wars...maybe that would solve overpopulation," I personally find these statements, even made in jest, to be disgusting. The continued presence of the hydro-gen bomb and our ongoing wars are themselves a disgrace to our species and should be stopped! There is no doubt that improvements in world health care has upped our population, but there is also no doubt that it is one of our greatest accomplishments. Thus we certainly don't want to alter that as we move to eliminate overpopulation.

Some people say the problem is our **over-consumption**. They feel that if we dealt with consumption by doing things like recycling or finding new technologies to provide more food, we could help to solve overpopulation. I am certainly not opposed to any of these things, but I don't really believe that they alone can stop, or even meaningfully effect, overpopulation. Certainly our arrogant abuse of the Earth and its plants and animals should be stopped, but in our present overpopulated condition that is fed by our towering greed and selfishness, it is impossible for even this to make any real difference.

Let me caution that some people try to address overpopulation on a **national level**. They seem to think that their nation can solve this problem by themselves and by cutting themselves off from everybody else. They ignore the fact that nations are just lines somebody drew on a map of the Earth, and that everything on the Earth is interconnected. Selfishly and cruelly they even say that stopping immigration and closing their borders will help their nation deal with overpopulation. Of course that is total nonsense. Our real home and citizenship belongs to the one Earth. This means that overpopulation can only be addressed in a global, world-wide way that includes every person and every group (including every nation). Unless we can do that, nothing will ever be done to stop it.

There is only one very obvious way to really solve this. The obvious thing that is causing overpopulation is having **too many children. Only by limiting the number of children each couple can have will we be able to stop this growing problem.** This solution could not be more simple to say, but it could not be more complicated to do. However there really is nothing more to say... **we must find a way do this!** If we don›t, our species will soon be extinct. The Earth and its ecosystems are already breaking down, but with even more population on the Earth, all of us will soon know what thirst and starvation means.

B. How Can We Accomplish This Solution?

Motivating couples to have just one child is not an easy thing to address. As I said, it will involve changes in the world's cultures, religions and expectations. Many people will need to look again at what marriage means and even what life is all about. For instance it will have to be accepted that the goal of life for a reflective, evolved species is not having children or being rich; the goal of reflective beings on this Earth needs to be advancing our evolution and the evolution of everyone and everything, (including the Earth and cosmos). Also our goal as interconnected, cosmic beings must also be to connect, to appreciate and to love all that is within us and around us. Of course it would also be to end this unsustainable overpopulation so it doesn't destroy us and much that is around us. To do this, we must all be participating in the one thing that is necessary to stop this disaster...limiting couples to having just one child.

I

This will include needed laws to be passed on a world-wide scale *requiring* all people to have one child. However the question still looms as to how we could ever enforce these laws. I believe that the first thing we will have to do is ***educate everyone* about overpopulation and what it means for the future of our species** on this planet. This education is necessary for *everyone,* so they can see and be on board with why they should have only one child. This is necessary because laws are only followed when the majority of people believe in them.

Do we do what many are already doing and disperse ***contraceptive devices*** to everyone to prevent pregnancy? Right now, many young people in the world have no idea about the complexities of sex and reproduction. They follow their natural instincts to suddenly find themselves mothers and fathers. They find themselves with huge responsibilities and demands that are over their heads. With contraceptive devices and some education about the results of pregnancy and being a parent, many pregnancy (especially in third world countries) can be avoided. The same is true for dealing with overpopulation. If people can be educated to understand how they can keep from having pregnancies, and what we are doing to the Earth and its ecosystems through our overpopulation (as well as what it means for our future), perhaps they will be motivated to help in stopping this destructive, tragic mistake. I repeat, the education of everyone is crucial!

Also do we require every man and women who has had one child to undergo a ***medical procedure*** to prevent more pregnancies? This has bad connotations to us because it has been so horridly abused in the past. It has been forceably used to keep various groups of people, or even races and cultures, from reproducing. However in this situation, it would be used to enforce a law that would give our species a future. It is effective now when used by individuals to prevent future pregnancies. However here it would be used to help everybody be responsible for giving our species a chance to exist.

Also, as a last resort, do we require the thing that would be the most controversial? Do we require women who are pregnant with a second child to have an ***early term abortion***? This subject is extremely divisive because some people believe that a human-being is created when an egg is fertilized in the womb to form a one celled organism called a Zygote, and then when the cells come together to form an Embryo. I personally don't see how these early pregnancy life forms can be called a human-being. Yes, it is a life-form, but it is far from the advanced, complex life-form we call human. Thus, even though I appreciate and would want to protect all life-forms on the Earth, if the mother (who is a extremely complex life-form) is threatened, or if it would help to keep all of humanity from being destroyed, I would see an early pregnancy abortion as being a regrettable, but necessary, option. I realize that many see this as being radical, but the law of having just one child would have to be strictly enforced or it will fall apart and be useless. Thus what we're talking about here is the best of options. Clearly nothing about everyone having just one child is appealing or simple, but, in this case, it must be done. Hard and difficult things must be done to end overpopulation before it's too late.

Let me add that something else that would really help us to eliminate overpopulation would be encouraging **couples to have *no* children.** It may surprise you that many people are doing that now. I have known couples who've said that they have chosen not to have children for a variety of reasons. Some women didn't want them because they found birth to be too frightening, or because it might mess-up their bodies, or that it would threaten their work. Some couples have felt that having children was too expensive, too much trouble, or might destroy their life-style. I even have some friends who've decided not to have children so they could adopt children from all over the world and make a difference. One couple I knew sent out an announcement to their family and friends (like a birth announcement) that said they were *not* going to have children.

Thus it is clear that not everybody is caught up in this must-have-children mania. Still all of these people said their relatives and friends were constantly trying to talk them into changing their minds. It cannot be denied that everywhere in the world there are feelings that when people get married they naturally *should, or even must,* have children. Many of the world's people choose to have children that they mistreat and can't even feed. Yet they still condemn other couples who decide to do otherwise. There is no question that this will be a big problem. Convincing people to accept one child, or even no child, to stop overpopulation will be an enormous challenge.

II

However there are other monstrous problem to this which we have not addressed. I think the main reason the nations of the world will resist requiring couples to have just one child has to do with **money.** It has to do with an economy that is based around the need for more people to bring in more money to feed what we call "**progress**". This concept has become so ingrained in our cultures that for us to change would be monumental!

When we say that to avoid the tragedy of extinction, couples must have just one child, it will be said that it will threaten or destroy **the economy**. For instance, China tried to cut its population by requiring couples to have one child. However they found that it meant they had fewer and fewer productive young people to earn enough money to support the older people whose numbers were rising. They pulled out of it because it was labeled an economic disaster. The same thing would be true every-where if there were not some world-wide, concentrated study to find ways to address and avoid this problem. A solution would involve research and planning with the cooperation of all of the nations. As reflective beings, we would be fully able to do that if we really tried.

III

Of course if all of that is hard, the results of *not* having one child, and *continuing with our overpopulation*, will be much, much harder! For instance, with no drinking water from glaciers or clean rivers and streams, with no food from the plants and animals we've killed off, no fish or marine life from the poisoned freshwater and seas, and with everyone fighting to find food and water to stay alive, total chaos, devoid of any law or order, will break out. All of this means that our overpopulated, crowded and *miserable relatives* will reach hard, tragic deaths. Of course at that time, **they** won't be able to do anything to avoid it, however right now **we** can! We should and must be wise and brave enough to keep this horrible scenario from happening to those who follow us by finding ways to limit every couple to one child. In the first generation with everyone participating, our population numbers will be cut in half! In several generations, if couples at that time could limit their children to two, there will be no more problem. It's as simple as that, but can we hear it? Can we do it?

C. Can it be done?

I

Of course nobody knows the answer to this question. I certainly don't know. However I do think that if enough people can face up to all the facts of our predicament, and if they are then able to assimilate these facts enough to do something, it definitely *can be done*. I believe that in spite of our many mistakes and blunders, we are still an intelligent species. For instance, if we can gather together the best minds that we have on the economy, I see no reason why they couldn't find some ways to lessen the economic impact.

I'm also sure we can find a way for all of the nations to cooperate and weather the storm of advancing what we mean by the word "progress". While we're at it, we could also design a new universal and just trade system involving all nations with their businesses, banks, stock markets or whatever that would be to the benefit of everyone. I am no economist, but I am convinced that just as we evolved into this present economic system in only few years, we could also rationally and quickly evolve another one. It would be a world economic system that would allow us to reverse overpopulation and and still be solvent in ways that would be much better for everyone.

Of course another of the biggest of these problems may lie in the fact that nothing can be done to solve human overpopulation until ***every nation*** in the world is on board, The people of all nations would need to be ready to make the sacrifices needed for a plan to succeed. I don't see how this can be until we wake up and see the tremendous threat of overpopulation. We would also need to face many other world problems that can only be solved with a fully representative, democratic, well funded and accepted **world government.** We would need that so we could pass and enforce laws on a world-wide scale. This is the only thing I can see that would alter and stop this insanity, as well as so many other problems (like our present wars, hydrogen bomb threats, the tragedy of wandering refugees, massive starvation, and universal health needs). I fully believe that if we had such a world governing body that was fully aware of overpopulation's problems, we could solve it. If overpopulation could be addressed from a world perspective, the needed laws could be passed, but without a world governing body, the chaos of prideful, self-centered actions of nations (which we now know all too well) will wipe away any road to a meaningful solution. Wouldn't it be wonderful if the realization of our overpopulation could be the thing that would motivate all of the nations of the world to put aside their divisive national pride and move into the reality of lasting peace and a future.

II

However there are some positive, hopeful things that can be said. It only took us 150 years to reach this point, and it will only take us 4 or 5 generations to return our population to the estimated sustainable number of 750 million. (This number of sustainability has been debated. Some people have said that rather than 750 million, it is as much as two and a half billion, or as few as 200 million. All I can say is that from my studies, I believe it to be around 750 million which is I think the number of our population that would allow other life forms to flourish.) Remember if all the people in the world had just one child, our population would go from 10 billion to 5 billion in just *one* generation. Thus we are not talking about a one-child limitation going on forever, Of course even after that we would still need to have a two-child requirement to keep overpopulation from happening all over again. However since nobody after this one child rule will ever want to face this problem again, having two children might not be difficult to enforce.

Also I was surprised to see that ten years ago the majority of couples in the US had children, but now 57% *do not* have children! (I really thought that most couples had children.) I think this statistic is amazing and will make the one child requirement, or even the no child suggestion much easier to accomplish, because 57% of the couples in the US will not even be affected. Even though statistics on a world-wide scale are hard to find, we can guess that something like this is happening all over the world.

III

So, yes we can stop our overpopulation of the Earth to avoid our species' extinction...just as we can also reverse our cruel treatment of plants, animals, marine life and the Earth itself. We can do it if we are willing to make some sacrifices that are minuscule in relation to the long-term results. It would also require us to make changes in our pride, selfishness and being stuck in only ourselves to discard the future. We would have to wake-up and work together with our fellow humans everywhere to stop our suicidal practices. We would have to accept our interconnected state and rejoice in being a part of the Earth and the cosmos to work for the good of all.

VI. Will We Stop It?

The question is not *can* we stop overpopulation. No, the real question is *will* we stop it. No one can answer to that, because no one can tell the future. Also since this discussion began, only a very few people have been motivated to learn anything about overpopulation. This means that almost no one is discussing it, and that does not bode well for the future. That's why I, and others, are writing a book about overpopulation, because regardless of the outcome, somebody has got to do something.

I was brought up on a beach in North Carolina, and I repeatedly had a nightmare. It was about when I was walking on the beach in front of my house and I looked up to see a huge tidal-wave coming in toward me. All I could do was turn and run as fast as I could to try to tell my parents to save them. I feel much the same way about this. I see this terrible reality looming on the horizon, and all I can do is cry out in writing to save my future relatives and my species. Of course there is one thing that is different in my dream...there I was alone...but now I am not. New people every-day are speaking out on this subject as they see what's happening, realize the truth about overpopulation, and feel a need to do something. As I said, numerous books, in addition to this one, are being written on this critical subject. One of my favorites is called Beyond Malthus by Brown, Gardner, and Halwell.

Robert Malthus lived from 1776 to 1834. In 1798, he is thought to be the first person to write about overpopulation . He saw that the increase in food production was leading to a population growth that was reducing the standard of living and was increasingly bringing hardship, suffering, want, famine and disease to the lower classes. He wrote, "The power of population is indefinitely greater than the power in the Earth to produce subsistence for man." He was ridiculed by his peers who at that time believed that society was increasingly evolving forward and would easily find ways to deal with this problem.

The present-day book Beyond Malthus moves the discussion about Population growth to the modern day as it talks about things like grain production, fresh water, biodiversity, energy, marine life, jobs, diseases, crops, forests, housing, urbanization, waste, meat production, income, and conflict. If you are still not convinced that overpopulation is a real threat, please read this book ,or another one like it, to get more information, because it really makes no sense for anyone to doubt this anymore. In this book, I am briefly trying to sound the alarm of its presence and consequences, but other longer books can offer you more facts and figures.

Since Malthus broke the ice, more and more scientists have spoken out. Recently **15,000 scientists**, writing in the Online International Journal Bio-science, have released a warning about our catastrophic future with overpopulation. It updates a warning by 1,700 scientists twenty-five years ago. It says that we are still facing the threat of our runaway consumption of limited world resources by our rapidly growing population. It says that nobody is doing enough to fight it, and if we don't act now, massive biodiversity will be lost with untold human misery. We must start recognizing in our day to day lives and in our governing institutions, that the Earth, together with all of its life-forms, is our only, true home.

The fact that our species is already moving into *extinction has become more and more accepted.* This is because it is obvious. Our selfish abuse of the Earth with its animals, plants and interconnected ecosystems, together with our mindless pollution of the air, rivers, oceans, and land make our extinction necessary.

This is already accepted by almost all environmentalists today. It has been accepted far more than the fact of our overpopulation. Almost nobody knows how much our numbers are growing to dramatically speed up our move into extinction. Obviously as more and more people abuse the ecosystems, the time we have left gets shorter and shorter. Thus it has become clear to those who have actually studied overpopulation, that it is a major player in our pending demise. Having addressed our abuse of the Earth and the resulting extinction in depth in my other books, I decided in this one to focus only on our overpopulation. I have tried to make it clear that not only is it contributing to our species extinction; it is a huge major player in this approaching horror. We now know that to talk about unchecked overpopulation is to talk about our extinction. We've come to see that these two subjects are two sides of the same coin, and unless we can stop overpopulation soon, we will never have enough time to stop our pollution and the annihilation of the ecosystems.

CONCLUSION

If each one of us can step-up bravely to face this, and if each one of us can start talking about it to convince other people to face it, maybe more people will pull their heads out of the sand and begin to do something. Perhaps they will be able to see how overpopulating our mother Earth is destroying the ecosystems that carry life.

Maybe they will even be able to face our absurd evolution into pride, greed and selfishness to disconnect with everything to blindly overpopulate the Earth. Maybe they will see that we have *lost* the natural force in the cosmos that is pulling us together (that I call "The Cosmic Way"), which is *moving us apart* in pride's unnatural hate, fear, anger, distrust and violence. If we can begin to face these things, we will soon regain our inner and outer peace and have a future to healthily evolve into the cosmos. This means that in spite of today's pessimistic condition, there is

still some hope for a supposedly intelligent species to recover...
and there really may be a way out of this mess.

Overpopulation leading to our extinction should not be
seen as some Armageddon or end-of-the-world theory. No, it is
simply a scientific, logical *fact* that can no more be covered up
and ignored by our escapes. Perhaps it's time to give up our lies
and superstitions to be who we really are, doing what we have to
do. We have to stop overpopulation from being seen as a casual
conversation piece to nod toward and then forget. We certainly
need to stop using it to rebel, as a way to be different, be liberal,
or be a part of some movement that may have some cool folks in
it. If we just wallow around in this swamp of meaningless noise,
nothing will happen...and it will be too late. The truth is that
only ***now*** can we do something about overpopulation, so ***now*** we
must wake up and act!

We do have some specific, logical options. (However that
means nothing when only meaningless noise rules the day.) For
instance, we can work to educate people about overpopulation's
reality, and what it is doing to this sacred Earth that is our home.
We can fight the escapes, cover-ups and the lies that people use
to discredit the massive evidence. We can help to reduce the fear

that overpopulation generates, such as its threat to our perceived wealth born out of progress. We can work to establish the idea that if every couple can have just one child, in a few generations there will be no problem. Perhaps we can also work to form a real, representative, democratic, strong United Nations organization that can pass laws on this and other things, and then enforce them. We can even work to curb the pride, greed, exclusiveness, fear, anger, hate, judgementalism, hoarding, injustice and violence that is tearing us apart to leave us devoid of uniting compassion and love.

We have to see that it's time to stand up and be counted. Other scientists, together with sensitive and aware people and groups (like "Population Control"), can help us if we let them. However we are the ones who have to be willing to be different and occasionally be laughed at, ridiculed, or totally ignored. That's not comfortable, but then the truth is not always comfortable. However the truth is always honest and the truth is always real. The truth is the most valuable thing we as humans have to struggle to improve ourselves and be who we really are. It is within this struggle for truth that we will find our path we must follow to address this monster that is stalking us...that we call overpopulation.

The alarm is being sounded. The call to action is clear. The future cries out to us. The question is can I, can you, can we, hear it and respond?

www.ingramcontent.com/pod-product-compliance
Lightning Source LLC
Chambersburg PA
CBHW031351060726
47590CB00007B/2729